50 Easy Mexica

Quick and Delicious Mexican Recipes

Table of contents

Chicken Enchiladas 5

Mexican Shrimp Cocktail 7

Mexican Tuna Stuffed Avocado 10

Skillet Chicken Tacos 12

Loaded Nachos 14

Cilantro Lime Chicken Taco 17

Chicken Quesadillas 19

Chili Con Carne 21

Fiesta Fajitas 24

Mexican Brown Rice 27

Mexican Beef Pizza 29

Mexican Burgers 31

Black Bean Burgers 33

Black Bean Burritos 35

Mexican Fried Potatoes and Bacon 38

Mexican Mini Tarts 40

Layered Taco Salad 42

Creamy Mexican Shrimp Pasta 44

Mexican Street Corn 47

Fresh Mexican Corn Soup 49

Mexican Rice	52
Mexican Beef Nachos	54
Ground Beef Enchiladas	57
Mexican Picadillo	59
Mexican Casserole	62
Mexican Shrimp Rice	65
Mexican Tartine	68
Mexican Chilaquiles Rojos	70
Couscous Stuffed Peppers	72
Mexican Quinoa	74
Mexican Style Lasagna	76
Mexican Pico De Gallo	78
Taco Casserole	80
Mexican Trash	82
Hearty Mexican Spaghetti	84
Mexican Buddha Bowl	86
Mexican Meatloaf	88
Mexican DIY Burrito Bowls	90
Mexican Flatbread	93
Mexican Shrimp Tacos	95
Corn and Chorizo Chowder	97
Mexican Frittata	99

Mexican Chicken and Rice 102

Mexican Hotdogs 105

Mexican Summer Couscous 107

Mexican Pozole 109

Mexican Chili-Lime Beef 112

Mexican Rotisserie Pizza 114

Mexican Corn Bread 116

Mexican Cheese Vegetable Chowder 118

Chicken Enchiladas

Prep Time:	10 minutes	Calories:	259
Cook Time:	20 minutes	Fat (g):	17
Total Time:	30 minutes	Protein (g):	28
Servings:	6	Net carbs:	14

Take the rotisserie breast meat, chop it, and fill up your tortillas with the delicious enchilada sauce.

Ingredients:

- Tortillas	Six
- Cooked chicken, chopped	2 cups
- Enchiladas sauce	1 ½ cup
- Cilantro, chopped	½ cup
- Green chilies	14 ounces
- Salt	½ tsp
- Black pepper	¼ tsp
- Cheddar cheese	2 cups
- Crumbled queso fresco	1 cup
- Sour cream, optional	

Instructions:

1. Preheat oven to 375 F.
2. Mix chicken, 1 cup enchilada sauce, green chilies, cilantro, queso fresco, salt, and pepper, and one cup cheddar cheese.
3. Place an equal portion of filling in each tortilla and roll.
4. Place in a greased baking dish and spoon remaining sauce and sprinkle the remaining cheese on top.
5. Bake for 15-20 minutes.

Tip: You can use the cheese of your choice. Serve with enchilada sauce.

Serving suggestion: Serve it as a complete meal and with avocado, green onions, lettuce, or lime.

Mexican Shrimp Cocktail

Prep Time:	20 minutes	Calories:	287
Cook Time:	15 minutes	Fat (g):	21
Total Time:	35 minutes	Protein (g):	28
Servings:	4	Net carbs:	11

With some real tomato juice, you can make this delicious cocktail that is going to be a perfect dinner for you.

Ingredients:

- Cooked Shrimp — 1 pound
- Salt — To taste
- Red onions — 1 cup
- Diced cucumber — 1 cup
- Chopped celery — ½ cup
- Minced jalapeno — One
- Freshly chopped tomatoes with their juices — 1 ½ cup
- Ketchup — ½ cup
- Chopped cilantro — ¼ cup
- Lime juice — 2 tbsp
- Hot sauce — To taste
- Avocado, cut in chunks — One

Instructions:

1. In a pot, boil salted water and add in shrimp and cook for 2-4 minutes. Take out shrimp. Reserve a cup of cooking water and chill it.
2. Now cut half shrimp in large chunks and leave the other half whole.
3. Place the chopped shrimp in a bowl and add in onions, cucumber, jalapeno, tomatoes, ketchup, cilantro, celery, hot sauce, and lime juice. Mix and set aside to chill.
4. Once the cooking water is at room temperature, add it to the shrimp cocktail a little at a time until you get the desired consistency. Place whole shrimp in a cocktail and arrange some on top.

Tip: Add salt and hot sauce for adjusting the taste.

Serving suggestion: Serve it as a main meal in bowls along with tortilla chips.

Mexican Tuna Stuffed Avocado

Prep Time:	10 minutes	Calories:	240
Cook Time:	0 minutes	Fat (g):	16
Total Time:	10 minutes	Protein (g):	12
Servings:	8	Net carbs:	5

The stuffed avocados bring tuna, black beans, veggies, and other spices together and give you a healthy lunch.

Ingredients:

- Hass avocados — 4, halves
- Albacore tuna in water — 2 5 ounces cans
- Black beans — ½ cup
- Dice tomatoes — One
- Red onion, chopped — ¼ cup
- Red bell pepper, chopped — ½ cup
- Diced jalapenos — 1
- Fresh cilantro — ¼ cup
- Juiced lime — 2 tbsp
- Cumin — 1 tsp
- Black pepper — 1/8 tsp

Instructions:

1. Combine tuna with beans, tomatoes, onion, bell pepper, jalapeno, lime juice, cilantro, cumin, and pepper in a bowl.
2. Remove the pit from the avocado and spoon a larger hole and stuff in tuna mixture.
3. Garnish with cilantro.

Tip: Serve with crumbled cheese.

Serving suggestion: Serve it as the main meal for dinner with sour cream if you want.

Skillet Chicken Tacos

Prep Time:	10 minutes	Calories:	330
Cook Time:	20 minutes	Fat (g):	10
Total Time:	30 minutes	Protein (g):	37
Servings:	6	Net carbs:	17

Boneless chicken thighs can be the perfect filling for your tacos. Enjoy your lunch or at dinner time and satisfy your cravings for soft tacos.

Ingredients:

- Fresh boneless chicken thighs — Four
- Taco seasoning mix — 1 ¼ ounce divided
- Water — 1/3 cup
- Flour tortillas — Six
- Refried beans — ½ cup
- Shredded Mexican cheese blend — 1 cup

Instructions:

1. Preheat oven to 400 F.
2. Cut chicken in half-inch cubes and sprinkle 1 tbsp of taco seasoning on the chicken.
3. Cook the seasoned chicken in oiled skillet and keep stirring for 4-5 mins.
4. Now add in water and remaining seasoning and let it boil.
5. Reduce heat and let cook for 5 minutes.
6. Spread the beans on tortillas and then place the chicken mixture on them all.
7. Top with cheese and fold to cover.
8. Place in a baking sheet and bake for 5 minutes. Serve.

Tip: If you prefer, you can sprinkle the chopped cilantro over the tacos. You can add corn on the tortilla to add flavor.

Serving suggestion: Serve it as the main meal for dinner with green onion garnishing.

Loaded Nachos

Prep Time:	10 minutes	Calories:	279
Cook Time:	20 minutes	Fat (g):	19.7
Total Time:	30 minutes	Protein (g):	9.5
Servings:	4	Net carbs:	17.2

Who does not love nachos and their crunchy taste? In this recipe, this Mexican loaded nachos dish is made with some simple steps and easy-to-find ingredients.

Ingredients:

- Ground chicken — 1 pound
- Olive oil — 1 tbsp
- Chili powder — 1 tsp
- Cumin — 1 tsp
- Coriander — 1 tsp
- Garlic powder — ½ tsp
- Dried oregano — ½ tsp
- Salt — 1 tsp
- Black pepper — To taste
- Corn tortilla chips — 16 ounces
- Black beans — 15 ounces
- Shredded Mexican cheese blend — 1 pound
- Tomatoes — Two
- Red onion — ¼
- Jalapeno chilies — One
- Cilantro leaves — ¼ cup
- Avocado — One
- Sliced black olives — 2 tbsp
- Lime — ½
- Sour cream — 1/3 cup

Instructions:

1. Preheat oven to 400 F. Line a baking sheet with parchment paper and set aside.
2. In a large skillet, drizzle some olive oil and let it shimmer a bit. Then add chicken and cook for 4-6 minutes. Keep breaking up the chicken with a spatula.
3. Add in spices with salt and pepper. Mix well.
4. Add black beans to the chicken and cook for a couple of minutes.
5. In the baking sheet, arrange the tortilla chips and cover with chicken and beans mixture. Leave a 1-inch border of chips uncovered.
6. Sprinkle the cheese evenly.
7. Place the baking sheet in the preheated oven and bake for 10-12 minutes until the cheese melts down.
8. Dice tomatoes and red onions and minced jalapeno chilies. Dice the avocados and chop the cilantro.
9. After removing nachos, top with diced tomatoes, onion, jalapeno, olives, avocado, and cilantro. Serve with sour cream topping.

Tip: If you prefer, you can squeeze lime juice over the topping.

Serving suggestion: Serve it as a complete meal and immediately.

Cilantro Lime Chicken Taco

Prep Time:	5 minutes	Calories:	154
Cook Time:	30 minutes	Fat (g):	3
Total Time:	35 minutes	Protein (g):	24
Servings:	8	Net carbs:	6

If you are a fan of slow cooking, then this cilantro lime chicken taco recipe is for you. With five ingredients, make this and enjoy tacos or tortillas.

Ingredients:

- Boneless chicken breasts   2 pounds
- Taco seasoning mix   1 packet
- Salsa jar   1 - 16 ounces
- Chopped fresh cilantro   1/3 cup
- Juice of two limes

Instructions:

1. Turn on the heat under a medium-sized pot and add in chicken breasts. Sprinkle taco seasoning over the top.
2. Cook for 30 minutes on medium-high heat. Keep stirring occasionally.
3. Remove chicken from the pot and shred with a fork. Cover with salsa, cilantro, then add lime juice to adjust moisture in the chicken. It's ready to serve.

Tip: Serve with taco shells or tortillas.

Serving suggestion: Serve it as a complete meal and with avocado, tomatoes, cheese, or sour cream.

Chicken Quesadillas

Prep Time:	10 minutes	Calories:	176
Cook Time:	10 minutes	Fat (g):	8.5
Total Time:	20 minutes	Protein (g):	12.5
Servings:	4	Net carbs:	11

Ingredients:

• Shredded jack cheese	1 cup
• Shredded cheddar cheese	1 cup
• 10-inch flour tortillas	Four
• Shredded cooked chicken	1 ½ cup
• Chopped cilantro	2 tbsp
• Guacamole	Optional
• Salsa	For serving
• Sour cream	For serving

Instructions:

1. Combine cheese in a bowl and set aside.
2. Preheat a large pan for 3 minutes and then place a tortilla on it.
3. Spread half chicken, half cilantro, and half cheese and top with the second tortilla and cook until the tortilla is brown on the bottom side.
4. Now flip the tortilla carefully and cook on the other side for 3 minutes.
5. Place the tortilla on a plate and cut in wedges.
6. Serve.

Serving suggestion: Serve it as a complete meal with guacamole, salsa, or sour cream.

Chili Con Carne

Prep Time:	10 minutes	Calories:	380
Cook Time:	30 minutes	Fat (g):	15
Total Time:	40 minutes	Protein (g):	28
Servings:	6	Net carbs:	35

Chili con carne is everyone's favorite dish, and this is a super exciting and yummy food for your lunch or dinner.

Ingredients:

- Ground beef — 1 pound
- Salt — 1 tsp
- Ground black pepper — ½ tsp
- Celery salt — ½ tsp
- Dijon mustard — 1 tsp
- Worcestershire sauce — 1 tsp
- Paprika paste — 2 tsp
- Ground cumin — 1 tsp
- Sliced red chilies — Four
- White onion — One
- Garlic cloves — Three
- Dark beer — 2 cups
- Crushed tomatoes — 28 ounces
- Black beans — 14 ounces
- Corn — 14 ounces

Instructions:

1. Crush garlic and remove the skin. Leave cloves in one piece. Slice the onion.
2. Mix the beef with pepper, salt, celery salt, Worcestershire sauce, paprika paste, mustard, cumin, and chilies.

3. Heat oil in a large pot and fry onions until soft. Add in garlic cloves and, after one minute, increase the heat and add in the beef. Divide the meat into small pieces and fry until nicely brown.
4. Deglaze the pan with beer and let simmer for 1 minute.
5. Add the diced tomatoes and stir it. Simmer for 15 minutes.
6. Drain black beans and corn and throw them in the pot.
7. Let cook for a few minutes and remove from heat.

Tip: If you prefer, you can sprinkle the chopped cilantro over the chili. Top with shredded cheese or avocado.

Serving suggestion: Serve it as a main meal for dinner with sour cream.

Fiesta Fajitas

Prep Time:	15 minutes	Calories:	234
Cook Time:	4 hours	Fat (g):	15
Total Time:	4 hours 15 minutes	Protein (g):	26
Servings:	4	Net carbs:	5

This is a quick and easy recipe. You can make the marinade ahead and keep it in the fridge!

Ingredients:

- flank steak — 1 pound
- onion — 1
- tomato — 1
- green bell pepper — 1

For the Fajita Marinade:

- garlic — 2 cloves
- Worcestershire sauce — 1 Tablespoon
- water — 1/2 cup
- lemon juice — 1/2 cup
- oregano — 1/2 teaspoon
- cumin — 1/2 teaspoon
- brown sugar substitute — 2 teaspoons
- Dash of Tabasco® sauce
- liquid smoke (optional) — 1/8 teaspoon
- bit of olive oil
- garnishes

Instructions:

1. Let's make the marinade first.
2. Crush the garlic; cut the green pepper into strips; cut the onion and the tomato into wedges. Combine all of the remaining ingredients for the marinade in a big glass bowl. Mix it up and make sure it is well blended.
3. Let's make the fajitas.

4. If you chose beef, then remove the fat you can see from the flank steak. Place the steak in a zippy and pour in the marinade.
5. Pop it in the fridge for at least 4 hours or overnight (if you're really after great flavor, overnight is the way to go).
6. Cut the steak into skinny strips and fry in a hot, non-stick skillet (with a bit of olive oil to prevent sticking). Do not allow the meat to overcook! When just about done, add the veggies and continue cooking until tender-crisp.
7. Serve with warmed tortillas and garnishes like shredded lettuce, sour cream, salsa, guacamole, tomatoes or any other favorites you would like.

Mexican Brown Rice

Prep Time:	5 minutes	Calories:	215
Cook Time:	10 minutes	Fat (g):	3.1
Total Time:	15 minutes	Protein (g):	7.8
Servings:	6	Net carbs:	41.5

Looking for an easy and simple recipe for Mexican rice? Get your hands on this amazing rice recipe with 5 ingredients, and it will be the most delicious rice you will ever have in your lunch or dinner.

Ingredients:

• Fresh or frozen corn	1 ½ cup
• Black beans	15 oz. can
• Whole grain brown rice	3 cups
• Chili powder	1 tbsp
• Salsa, homemade or jarred	1 cup
• Fresh cilantro and avocados	For garnish

Instructions:

1. Over medium heat, preheat a large size pan or skillet and add in beans and corn. Cook for 2-3 minutes until tender.
2. Now add in rice and chili powder and mix well.
3. Keep stirring for 3 minutes. Then add salsa and cook for two more minutes until it's warm enough.
4. Remove from heat, let cool and serve.

Tip: If you prefer, you can top it with sliced avocados, tomatoes and cilantro. You can also layer the ingredients cooked separately in a casserole and serve.

Serving suggestion: Serve it as a main meal or along with tacos or enchiladas. It is also perfect for burrito filling.

Mexican Beef Pizza

Prep Time:	10 minutes	Calories:	310
Cook Time:	20 minutes	Fat (g):	16
Total Time:	30 minutes	Protein (g):	19
Servings:	6	Net carbs:	22

Make this simple and amazing pizza at home and enjoy the best Mexican food experience.

Ingredients:

• Ground beef	½ pound
• Taco seasoning	3 tbsp
• Refried beans	½ cup
• Salsa	½ cup
• Shredded taco blend cheese	½ cup
• 10-inch flour tortilla	Two
• Topping of choice	

Instructions:

1. Preheat oven to 350 F.
2. Brown the meat in a skillet and add taco seasoning. Mix well.
3. Place a tortilla on the baking sheet and top with beans, then meat, and place the other tortilla on it.
4. Bake for 10 minutes and then spread salsa and cheese on top.
5. Bake for 6-10 minutes again and serve.

Tip: You can use cheese of your choice for topping.

Serving suggestion: Serve it as a complete meal and enjoy with ketchup or a favorite sauce.

Mexican Burgers

Prep Time:	10 minutes	Calories:	430
Cook Time:	10 minutes	Fat (g):	30
Total Time:	20 minutes	Protein (g):	36
Servings:	4	Net carbs:	2

Do you get excited by the word "burgers"? If yes, then you must try this ultimate tasty burger having ground beef filled with cheese and topped with some great veggies.

Ingredients:

- Ground beef — 1 ½ pound
- Ground cumin — 1 tbsp
- Chili powder — ½ tsp
- Onion powder — ½ tsp
- Garlic powder — ¼ tsp
- Salt — ¼ tsp
- Jack cheese with hot chili peppers — 4 slices

Instructions:

1. Place the ground beef in a bowl and mix all seasoning ingredients together.
2. Form 8 equal-size patties.
3. Place cheese slices on 4 patties and place the other 4 over each.
4. Press the edges together to seal.
5. Grill over hot coals or broil and take off once done.

Tip: You can place them in hamburger buns and also layer with sliced tomatoes, salad leaves, and onions.

Serving suggestion: Serve it as a main meal along with fries and your favorite soda.

Black Bean Burgers

Prep Time:	10 minutes	Calories:	227
Cook Time:	35 minutes	Fat (g):	10
Total Time:	45 minutes	Protein (g):	8
Servings:	4	Net carbs:	25

These burgers are really easy to make and are delicious and healthy at the same time. Enjoy the tastes of Mexican food right at your home from your own kitchen.

Ingredients:

- Mashed avocado — 1 cup
- Lime juice — 2 tbsp
- Black beans, rinsed and drained — 15 ounces
- Salt — ¼ tsp
- Garlic powder — ¼ tsp
- Chia seeds — 1 tbsp
- Minced jalapeno — ¼ cup
- Chopped green onion — ¼ cup
- Quick oats — ¼ cup
- Olive oil — 1 tbsp
- Chopped cilantro, for serving, optional — 2 tbsp
- Salsa, for serving, optional — ¼ cup

Instructions:

1. Take a bowl and mix the mashed avocados with lime juice.
2. Add half of the beans with garlic powder and salt. Mash them.
3. Add in chia seeds, jalapeno, onions, oats, and remaining beans and mix well.
4. Form four patties from the mixture and let rest for at least a half-hour.
5. Heat oil in a pan and add in patties and cook for 5-8 minutes on both sides until they are crispy.

Tip: If you prefer, you can sprinkle the chopped cilantro.

Serving suggestion: Serve it as the main meal for dinner with salsa.

Black Bean Burritos

Prep Time:	20 minutes	Calories:	387
Cook Time:	10 minutes	Fat (g):	18
Total Time:	30 minutes	Protein (g):	12
Servings:	4	Net carbs:	35

These burritos are made with rice, beans, and guacamole. They are easy to make and make your dinner super delicious and amazing.

Ingredients:

<u>Guacamole:</u>

- Avocados — Two
- Minced red onions — ¼ cup
- Minced cilantro — ¼ cup
- Minced garlic clove — One
- Lime — One
- Salt — ¼ tsp

<u>Burrito:</u>

- Whole wheat tortilla, large — Two
- Cooked brown rice — ½ cup
- Cooked black beans — ½ cup
- Shredded cheddar cheese — 1/3 cup
- Shredded lettuce — ½ cup
- Minced red onion — 3 tbsp

Instructions:

1. For the guacamole, cut the avocado in half and spoon out the flesh in a bowl.
2. Mash the avocado and add in onion, garlic, cilantro, and salt and squeeze the juice of half a lime in it.
3. Mix well and adjust the taste of lime.
4. Take a tortilla and spread guacamole on it. Now layer rice, cheese, beans, lettuce, and onions. Roll in burrito and tuck in the ends.
5. In a grill pan, place the burritos and cook on low heat until they are crispy.

Tip: You can use the cheese of your choice. If you want, you can skip the guacamole. The burrito will be perfect with beans and rice too.

Serving suggestion: Serve it as a complete meal and enjoy with salsa.

Mexican Fried Potatoes and Bacon

Prep Time:	5 minutes	Calories:	320
Cook Time:	15 minutes	Fat (g):	21
Total Time:	20 minutes	Protein (g):	10
Servings:	4	Net carbs:	23

You can enjoy the taste of potatoes and bacon with this simple and delicious dinner recipe. Make it easy in no time and have fun.

Ingredients:

• Potatoes	Two
• Bacon strips	3 – 6
• Onion	One
• Green chilies, minced	5 ounces
• Cumin	2 tsp
• Salt and pepper	To taste

Instructions:

1. Microwave your potatoes for 7 minutes on potato setting.
2. Fry bacon in a pan until crispy. Remove and reserve the dripping.
3. Cook onions in the reserved dripping until translucent. Add in green chilies and cook for 3 minutes.
4. Cut potatoes into bite-size pieces and add to the pan and cook until tender.
5. Season with cumin, salt, and pepper.

Tip: Top it with cheese or salsa if you want.

Serving suggestion: Serve it as a main meal. Also, use it for burrito filling and enjoy with eggs.

Mexican Mini Tarts

Prep Time:	15 minutes	Calories:	313
Cook Time:	30 minutes	Fat (g):	15
Total Time:	45 minutes	Protein (g):	14
Servings:	4	Net carbs:	36

For your perfect dinner, these tarts will be your favorite. Bringing black beans, corn, onions, and cheese and topping up with lime and avocados can be a perfect combination.

Ingredients:

- Masa flour — 2 cups
- Water — 1 ¾ cup
- Salt — 1 tsp
- Oil — For greasing
- Beef — ¾ pound
- Yellow onions, diced and sautéed — Half
- Back beans — 1 cup
- Corns — 1 cup
- Salsa — 1 cup
- Hot sauce — 2 tbsp
- Pickled jalapenos — ¾ cup
- Shredded cheddar cheese — 1 ½ cup
- Shredded white sharp cheddar — 1 ½ cup

Instructions:

1. Preheat oven to 350 F.
2. Combine flour with salt, make the dough, and set aside.
3. Grease the mini pie pans with oil and press masa dough in each. It should be thin like pizza dough.
4. Now spread beef, onions, beans, corn, jalapenos, salsa, and hot sauce into each mini pie pan.
5. Top with cheese and bake for 30 minutes in the preheated oven.

Tip: If you prefer, you can use avocado slices with lime for topping.

Layered Taco Salad

Prep Time:	20 minutes	Calories:	424
Cook Time:	10 minutes	Fat (g):	20
Total Time:	30 minutes	Protein (g):	27
Servings:	6	Net carbs:	25

Layered salad is one of the most exciting things to have in your dinner. Layering it with salsa, lettuce, tomatoes, corn, beans, avocados, yogurt, and tortilla chips will be the best thing.

Ingredients:

- Canola oil — 1 tbsp
- Lean ground turkey — 1 pound
- Chili powder — 2 tbsp
- Salt — ½ tsp
- Avocado — One
- Nonfat plain Greek yogurt — ½ cup
- Unsalted tortilla chips — 1 ½ cup
- Prepared salsa — 1 cup
- Pinto beans or corn — 15 ounces
- Romaine lettuce, thinly sliced — 5 cups
- Mexican cheese blend — ½ cup
- Chopped tomato — One

Instructions:

1. In a large skillet, cook turkey with chili powder and ¼ tsp of salt. Cook for 5 minutes or until done.
2. Mash avocado and mix with yogurt and remaining salt.
3. In a serving bowl, start layering. Place lettuce, avocado, salsa, yogurt, tomatoes, corn or beans, turkey, cheese, and tortilla chips.

Tip: You can use cheese of your choice and add any other ingredients you want.

Serving suggestion: Serve it as a complete meal. Layer the ingredients as per your desire.

Creamy Mexican Shrimp Pasta

Prep Time:	15 minutes	Calories:	206
Cook Time:	30 minutes	Fat (g):	9
Total Time:	45 minutes	Protein (g):	14
Servings:	4	Net carbs:	18

This Mexican dish will make you love it at your lunch or dinner times.

Ingredients:

- shrimp	1 pound
- fettuccine pasta	16 ounces
- butter	2 tbsp
- chili powder	¾ tsp
- sea salt	½ tsp
- red pepper flakes	A pinch
- cayenne	¼ tsp
- green chilies	17 ounces
- white wine	2 ounces (a splash for deglazing)
- lime	One
- avocado, diced	One

For sauce:

- Oaxaca cheese	8 ounces – reserve some for topping
- milk	1 cup
- chicken broth	12 ounces
- cayenne	¼ tsp
- red pepper flakes	A pinch
- salt	½ tsp

Instructions:

1. For pasta preparation, boil a large pot of water and cook pasta according to the packet instructions.
2. For the sauce, in a saucepan, warm up milk and add grated cheese gradually. Once the cheese is melted, mix the flour in ¼ cup of cold broth. Pour the mixture in cheese mixture and mix for a minute. Now add in remaining broth with remaining ingredients and cook well.
3. In a pan, melt 2 tbsp butter and add in shrimp seasoned with ¾ tsp chili powder, ½ tsp sea salt, ¼ tsp cayenne, a pinch of red pepper flakes.
4. Cook shrimp until pink and removes on a plate.
5. Deglaze the pan with wine and add green chilies, pasta, and cream sauce. Add in shrimp and give a stir.

Tip: Enjoy with avocados if you want.

Serving suggestion: Serve it as a complete meal with garlic bread and margaritas.

Mexican Street Corn

Prep Time:	5 minutes	Calories:	110
Cook Time:	30 minutes	Fat (g):	8
Total Time:	35 minutes	Protein (g):	5
Servings:	4	Net carbs:	6

Sweet Mexican corn is an amazing lunch item for the ones who want to enjoy some cheesy stuff. So, make it at home and enjoy it to the fullest.

Ingredients:

- Corn ears — Four
- Softened butter — 1 tbsp
- Mayonnaise — 1 tbsp
- Crumbled cheese of choice — ¼ cup
- Chili powder — To taste
- Chopped cilantro — 1 tbsp
- Lime — One

Instructions:

1. Cook corn with your preferred method. You can bake it in the oven for half an hour or grill it or boil it.
2. Now mix up the butter with mayonnaise and blend well.
3. Brush the butter mixture and sprinkle cheese with chili powder.

Tip: Coat the corn well with cheese if you want a full cheesy taste.

Serving suggestion: Serve it as the main meal with lime and chopped cilantro.

Fresh Mexican Corn Soup

Prep Time:	10 minutes	Calories:	202
Cook Time:	35 minutes	Fat (g):	12
Total Time:	45 minutes	Protein (g):	9
Servings:	4	Net carbs:	16

Mexican corn soup is a cozy and delicious dinner time food that you can make at home with some simple ingredients.

Ingredients:

- Fresh corn ears — Three
- Olive oil — 2 tsp
- Chopped red onion — ¼ cup
- Chicken or vegetable broth — 3 cups
- Milk — 1 cup
- Salt and pepper — To taste

<u>For garnishing:</u>

- Fresh cilantro
- Corns
- Crumbled cheese
- Lime wedges

Instructions:

1. In a bowl, slice the kernels from the corn ears using a sharp knife.
2. In a large soup pot, pour the oil at medium heat. Once the oil is hot, throw in onions. Cover a cook for a few minutes.
3. After 5 minutes, add in corn and broth and close the lid and let the corn cook. Once the mixture comes to a boil, reduce the heat and cook for 25 minutes.
4. Once the corn is cooked, blend the mixture with a hand blender until desired consistency.
5. Add in milk and salt and pepper and mix well. Top with desired toppings to serve.

Tip: If you prefer, you can squeeze lime juice over it and garnish with diced tomatoes.

Serving suggestion: Serve it as a complete meal and immediately.

Mexican Rice

Prep Time:	10 minutes	Calories:	200
Cook Time:	35 minutes	Fat (g):	4
Total Time:	45 minutes	Protein (g):	6
Servings:	5	Net carbs:	36

This simple rice is so delicious and easy to prepare with chicken broth and onions with simple spices.

Ingredients:

- Long grain white rice — 1 cup
- Chicken broth — 2 cups
- Olive oil — 1 tbsp
- Diced onion — One
- Minced garlic cloves — Four
- Tomato paste — ¼ cup
- Lime juice — 1 tbsp
- Chopped cilantro — ½ cup
- Cumin — 2 tsp
- Salt

Instructions:

1. In a cooking pot, add chicken broth with rice and bring to boil at high heat.
2. Mix and cover the pot, lower the heat and let cook on low for 18-20 minutes.
3. Remove from heat and keep aside for 5 minutes.
4. While rice is cooking, heat olive oil in a pan and cook onions in it. When they start to get brown, add in garlic and cook for a minute.
5. Now, add in tomato paste and cumin and cook for 2 minutes.
6. Season with salt and lime juice.

Tip: If you prefer, you can sprinkle the chopped cilantro and green onions.

Serving suggestion: Serve it as the main meal for dinner with your favorite curry.

Mexican Beef Nachos

Prep Time:	10 minutes	Calories:	417
Cook Time:	20 minutes	Fat (g):	24
Total Time:	30 minutes	Protein (g):	12
Servings:	4	Net carbs:	32

These Mexican nachos are loaded with beef, Mexican cheese, and cotija cheese with a lot of other items as well.

Ingredients:

- Diced white onion — Half
- Ground beef — ½ pound
- Ground cumin — 1 ½ tsp
- Ancho chili powder — 1 tsp
- Salt — 1 tsp
- Corn chips — 4 cups
- Black beans — 1 cup
- Mexican cheese — 2 cups
- Jalapeno — One
- Cotija cheese — 1 ounce
- Radish, sliced — Two
- Avocado, diced — Half
- Cilantro leaves — 1 handful

Instructions:

1. Preheat oven to 300 F.
2. In a pan, add oil and cook onions until translucent.
3. Now add ground beef and sprinkle cumin over it with chili powder and salt.
4. Cook for 5-8 minutes until beef is brown. Take off from heat and set aside.
5. Take a baking sheet and add a layer of chips. Top with beef, beans, and cheese.
6. Then layer another round of chips, beef, beans, and cheese.

7. Bake them for 10 minutes until cheese melts down.

Tip: You can make two to three layers as per your choice.

Serving suggestion: Serve it as a complete meal with jalapenos, Cotija cheese, radish, avocado, and cilantro.

Ground Beef Enchiladas

Prep Time:	5 minutes	Calories:	374
Cook Time:	25 minutes	Fat (g):	22
Total Time:	30 minutes	Protein (g):	20
Servings:	8	Net carbs:	12

They are the best beef enchiladas that will be ready in half an hour, and your family will love them for lunch or dinner.

Ingredients:

- Ground beef — 1 pound
- Diced yellow onion — One
- Taco seasoning — 1 tbsp
- Enchiladas sauce — 2 cups
- Tortillas — Eight
- Shredded cheddar cheese — 1 cup
- Shredded jack cheese — 1 cup

Instructions:

1. Preheat oven to 350 F.
2. Cook beef with onion and taco seasoning until no longer pink.
3. Drain the fat from beef and set aside.
4. Combine the cheese in a large bowl.
5. In a baking sheet, add half cup enchiladas sauce.
6. Place tortillas on a flat surface and spoon the ground beef and 1/8 cup cheese and roll them up.
7. Place the tortillas in a baking sheet and top with remaining enchiladas sauce and cheese and bake for 15-20 minutes.

Tip: You can use any other cheese you want.

Serving suggestion: Serve it as the main meal with jalapeno and green onions.

Mexican Picadillo

Prep Time:	15 minutes	Calories:	570
Cook Time:	40 minutes	Fat (g):	27
Total Time:	45 minutes	Protein (g):	41
Servings:	4	Net carbs:	38

Mexican picadillo is a quite satisfying and delicious dish you can easily make at home with your desired seasonings.

Ingredients:

- Fire-roasted tomatoes — 14 ounces
- Poblano peppers, chopped — Half
- Garlic cloves — Four
- Fresh cilantro — 1 bunch
- Onion cut in chunks — One
- Salt — 1 tsp
- Ground black pepper — ¼ tsp
- Diced yellow onion — One
- Diced garlic cloves — Four
- Tomato paste — 1 tbsp
- Bay leaves — Two
- Ground cumin — 2 tsp
- Dried oregano — 2 tsp
- Black pepper — To taste
- Dry white wine — ½ cup
- Ground beef — 1 ½ pound
- Chili powder — 2 tsp
- Yukon gold potatoes, diced — Two
- Diced carrots — Two

Instructions:

1. Place the roasted tomatoes with poblano pepper, the first portion of garlic cloves, first onions portion, and cilantro in a food processor and pulse to get salsa-like consistency.
2. Season with salt and pepper and set aside.
3. Sauté diced onions in oil for a few minutes and add in garlic and cook for 30 seconds.
4. Add in tomato paste, cumin, oregano, salt, bay leaves, and pepper and cook for 2 minutes.
5. Add wine and cook for 5 minutes.
6. Add in beef and season with chili powder, salt, pepper, and cumin and cook until beef starts to change color. Add in potatoes and carrots and sauté for a few minutes.
7. Add in the salsa mixture and combine well. Let cook it covered for 20-25 minutes on low heat.
8. Serve with garnish items.

Tip: You can use any remaining for stuffing bell peppers or roasted potatoes.

Serving suggestion: Serve it as a complete meal with grated cheese.

Mexican Casserole

Prep Time:	20 minutes	Calories:	299
Cook Time:	30 minutes	Fat (g):	10
Total Time:	50 minutes	Protein (g):	17
Servings:	8	Net carbs:	33

This cheesy casserole brings a lot of fun to your dinner with cheese, veggies, and tortillas.

Ingredients:

- Olive oil — 1 tbsp
- Minced garlic cloves — Two
- Diced onion — One
- Diced red bell pepper — One
- Diced green bell pepper — One
- Back beans — 15 ounces
- Roasted corn kernels — 1 cup
- Chili powder — 1 tsp
- Cumin — ½ tsp
- Salt and pepper — To taste
- Chopped green chilies — 4-5 ounces
- Chopped cilantro — 2 tbsp
- Whole-wheat tortillas, chopped — 4
- Refried beans, warmed — 16 ounces
- Mild enchiladas sauce — 10 ounces
- Low fat shredded Mexican cheese blend — 1 ½ cups

Instructions:

1. Preheat oven to 375 F.
2. In a large pan, heat oil and add garlic, onion, and bell peppers. Cook for 4 minutes.
3. Add in beans, corns, chili powder, and cumin and cook for 2 minutes.

4. Season with salt and pepper and add in green chilies with cilantro.
5. Place tortillas in a baking dish and spread refried beans, then onion mixture, and enchiladas sauce. Top with cheese.
6. Place in oven and bake for 18-20 minutes.
7. Serve immediately with cilantro.

Tip: You can add more vegetables if you want to.

Serving suggestion: Serve it as the main meal for dinner.

Mexican Shrimp Rice

Prep Time:	10 minutes	Calories:	492
Cook Time:	50 minutes	Fat (g):	7
Total Time:	60 minutes	Protein (g):	42
Servings:	4	Net carbs:	68

This Mexican rice recipe is simple, healthy and full of Mexican flavor spices.

Ingredients:

- extra virgin olive oil — 1 ½ tbsp
- shrimp — 1 pound
- chili powder — 1 ½ tsp
- garlic powder — 1 ½ tsp
- ground cumin — ¾ tsp
- salt — ½ tsp
- chopped yellow onions — 1
- chopped jalapenos — 2
- chopped red bell peppers — 2
- oregano — 1 tsp
- black pepper — ¼ tsp
- black beans — 15 ounces
- long-grain brown rice — 1 cup
- diced tomatoes in green chilies — 20 ounces
- water — 1 ½ cups
- green onions, chopped — Three
- chopped cilantro — ¼ cup
- lime cut in wedges — one

Instructions:

1. In a large pot, add 1 tbsp oil and add in shrimp. Add in ½ tsp chili powder, ½ tsp garlic powder, ¼ tsp cumin, and ¼ tsp salt. Mix well and cook for 2-3 minutes. Remove to a plate and set aside.
2. Add the remaining oil with onion, jalapeno, and bell peppers and cook for 5 minutes. Add oregano, black pepper, remaining chili powder, 1 tsp garlic powder, and ½ tsp cumin. Mix and cook for half a minute.
3. Add in rice and beans. Mix to coat well.
4. Add in tomatoes with juices and stir. Bring to boil, and the lower the heat and cook for 30 minutes.
5. Add in green onions, cilantro, reserved shrimp, and squeeze lime over them.

Tip: You can use sour cream or Greek yogurt for topping.

Serving suggestion: Serve it as a complete meal with avocados or sliced jalapenos.

Mexican Tartine

Prep Time:	5 minutes	Calories:	340
Cook Time:	20 minutes	Fat (g):	16
Total Time:	25 minutes	Protein (g):	15
Servings:	2	Net carbs:	27

With cheese, beans, and pork, make this open-faced sandwich with a Mexican twist.

Ingredients:

- Toasted Italian bread — 2 slices
- Pulled pork — 1 ½ cup
- Olive oil — 1 tbsp
- Garlic cloves — One, minced
- Black beans, cooked — 1 cup
- Diced jalapeno — Half
- Crumbled queso fresco — ½ cup
- Guacamole or avocado chunks — ½ cup

Instructions:

1. Preheat oven to 425 F.
2. In a saucepan, heat oil, then add garlic, and cook for a minute. Add in black beans and jalapeno. Cook for a couple of minutes. Remove from heat and mash the beans until smooth.
3. Spread the sliced bread with bean mixture, then top with pork, and bake for 7-10 minutes.
4. Add crumbled queso fresco and bake for 5 more minutes.
5. Remove and top with guacamole or avocado chunks as you like.

Tip: Top it with diced tomatoes if you want to add a twist.

Serving suggestion: Serve it as the main meal with your favorite salsa and hot sauce.

Mexican Chilaquiles Rojos

Prep Time:	10 minutes	Calories:	194
Cook Time:	20 minutes	Fat (g):	11
Total Time:	30 minutes	Protein (g):	6
Servings:	4	Net carbs:	27

This is a traditional Mexican dish that is a combination of chips for chilaquiles, and the Rojo is the salsa used with the chips.

Ingredients:

- Tortilla chips — 12 ounces

For salsa Rojo:

- Ripe tomatoes — 1 pound
- Garlic clove, minced — One
- White onion, sliced or chopped — ½
- Jalapeno or serrano chile — One
- Sea salt — ¾ tsp

For garnish:

- White onion, sliced or chopped — ¼ cup
- Crumbles queso fresco — ¼ cup
- Sour cream — ¼ cup

Instructions:

1. Place the vegetables in a baking sheet and heat in the oven broiler for 15 mins. Place the tomatoes, garlic, onion, and half chile with salt in a blender and make a puree.
2. Heat salsa Rojo in a skillet and stir over tortilla chips on a plate.

Tip: Serve right away if you like them crispy, and if soft, then wait for a few minutes.

Serving suggestion: Serve it as the main meal for dinner with sour cream, cilantro, queso fresco, cheese, and white onion.

Couscous Stuffed Peppers

Prep Time:	25 minutes	Calories:	85
Cook Time:	45 minutes	Fat (g):	4
Total Time:	1 hour 10 minutes	Protein (g):	6
Servings:	8	Net carbs:	7

These bell peppers are stuffed with couscous that can be enjoyed with your favorite toppings.

Ingredients:

- Whole-wheat couscous — 1 cup
- Bell peppers — Four
- Minced garlic cloves — Three
- Shredded parmesan cheese — 1 cup
- Salt and pepper — To taste

Instructions:

1. In a saucepan, add a cup of water and bring it to boil.
2. Remove from heat and add in the couscous with salt and pepper and stir. Let sit for 5 minutes.
3. Stain the couscous and mix with parmesan cheese and garlic.
4. Preheat oven to 350 F.
5. Cut the peppers in half, lengthwise. Remove stem and clean it up from seeds.
6. Fill all with the couscous mixture and place it on a baking sheet. Bake for 30 minutes or until peppers are done.

Tip: You can use more ingredients like onion, beans, or tomatoes if you want.

Serving suggestion: Serve it as a complete meal with guacamole, salsa, or avocado.

Mexican Quinoa

Prep Time:	15 minutes	Calories:	195
Cook Time:	15 minutes	Fat (g):	3
Total Time:	30 minutes	Protein (g):	8
Servings:	8	Net carbs:	31

With lime, tomatoes, onion, and quinoa, enjoy the night with your family.

Ingredients:

- Uncooked quinoa — 2 cups
- Chicken broth — 4 cups
- Chopped red onion — ½ cup
- Diced Roma tomatoes — Four
- Sliced jalapeno — One
- Lime juice — To taste
- Cilantro, chopped — A handful
- Salt and pepper — To taste

Instructions:

1. Cook quinoa in chicken broth for 15 minutes.
2. Place it in a dish and spread out and keep in a refrigerator for an hour.
3. Toss the cold quinoa with lime juice, tomatoes, onion, peppers, and cilantro.
4. Adjust salt and pepper and serve cold.

Tip: Store the leftover in an airtight jar for later use.

Serving suggestion: Serve it as a main meal in bowls along with lime wedges.

Mexican Style Lasagna

Prep Time:	20 minutes	Calories:	370
Cook Time:	30 minutes	Fat (g):	18
Total Time:	50 minutes	Protein (g):	30
Servings:	6	Net carbs:	18

Want to try lasagna in Mexican style? This is the perfect and simplest recipe to follow for the best lasagna ever!

Ingredients:

- Lean ground beef — 1 ½ pound
- Water — ¼ cup
- Salsa — ¾ cup
- Mexican Velveeta cheese — ¼ pounds, cut in cubes
- Flour tortilla — 6
- Shredded jack cheese — ½ cup

Instructions:

1. Preheat oven to 400 F.
2. Cook meat in a skillet and add in water and Velveeta until cheese melts.
3. Remove from heat and add in salsa.
4. Spray cooking spray in a baking dish and spread ¼ of meat in the bottom. Top with two tortillas and repeat with two layers.
5. Top with shredded cheese and bake for 30 minutes and serve.

Tip: You can add olives or beans in the layering.

Serving suggestion: Serve it as a complete meal with a crispy green salad.

Mexican Pico De Gallo

Prep Time:	10 minutes	Calories:	90
Cook Time:	0 minutes	Fat (g):	0
Total Time:	10 minutes	Protein (g):	4
Servings:	2	Net carbs:	12

This Pico de Gallo is a complete and healthy meal you can make in your kitchen in just 10 minutes.

Ingredients:

• Diced Roma tomatoes	6 cups
• Diced white onions	1 cup
• Jalapeno peppers	Four
• Chopped cilantro	¾ cup
• Lime juice	4 tbsp
• Salt	A pinch

Instructions:

1. Take a large bowl and add in tomatoes, onions, and jalapeno peppers.
2. Sprinkle cilantro and mix well. Add salt and lime juice.

Tip: Adjust salt as per your desire. You can use serrano peppers for spicy salsa.

Serving suggestion: Serve it as the main meal for dinner.

Taco Casserole

Prep Time:	10 minutes	Calories:	412
Cook Time:	20 minutes	Fat (g):	8
Total Time:	30 minutes	Protein (g):	46
Servings:	4	Net carbs:	45

This is the most delicious taco casserole that you can make in your kitchen with some easy-to-find ingredients.

Ingredients:

- Ground chicken breast — 1 pound
- Diced white onion — Half
- Whole kernel corn — 1 can
- Black beans — 1 can
- Taco seasoning — 1 tbsp
- Taco sauce — 2 tbsp
- Fat-free sour cream — ¼ cup
- Shredded cheddar cheese — ½ cup
- Diced fresh tomatoes — 1 cup
- Green onions — 1/3 cup

Instructions:

1. Sauté the meat with beans, onion, taco sauce, seasoning, and corn on medium heat in a pan until meat is brown.
2. Spoon half the meat mixture in the casserole and top with a layer of sour cream. Sprinkle cheese.
3. Repeat the same process of layering and bake for 15 minutes and serve.

Tip: You can use the cheese of your choice. Top with tomatoes and green onions.

Serving suggestion: Serve it as a complete meal and with sour cream.

Mexican Trash

Prep Time:	10 minutes	Calories:	320
Cook Time:	35 minutes	Fat (g):	23
Total Time:	45 minutes	Protein (g):	33
Servings:	4	Net carbs:	15

This Doritos casserole is such a great and amazing dish you can bake with some simple ingredients.

Ingredients:

- Doritos — 1 bag
- Shredded chicken — 2 cups
- Shredded cheese — 2 cups
- Cream of chicken soup — 1 can
- Tomatoes — 1 can
- Sour cream — ½ cup
- Milk — ½ cup
- Taco seasoning — ½ package

Instructions:

1. Preheat oven to 350 F.
2. With a nonstick spray, spray a casserole and set aside.
3. Mix all ingredients except Doritos and layer half of the Doritos on the bottom of the casserole and then spread half the chicken mixture.
4. Then layer the remaining Doritos and then the chicken mixture. Add more cheese on top and cover up with foil.
5. Bake for 35 minutes.

Tip: if you have a big casserole, double the recipe and bake for 45 minutes.

Serving suggestion: Serve it as the main meal.

Hearty Mexican Spaghetti

Prep Time:	10 minutes	Calories:	410
Cook Time:	20 minutes	Fat (g):	10
Total Time:	30 minutes	Protein (g):	29
Servings:	6	Net carbs:	59

The great fusion of Mexican items with Italian pasta brings a great meal to your table. Enjoy it with the best recipe.

Ingredients:

- Spaghetti pasta — 12 ounces
- Lean ground beef — 1 pound
- Taco seasoning mix — 1 ¼ ounce package
- Diced tomatoes — 14.5 ounces
- Whole kernel corn — 11 ounces
- Chopped green chilies — 7 ounces
- Sliced green onions — ½ cup
- Mexican cheese, shredded — ½ cup

Instructions:

1. Cook the spaghetti according to the instructions on package and drain.
2. Cook beef in a pan with seasoning and add in tomatoes, corn, green chilies, and onions. Cook until tender.
3. Add the mixture in spaghetti and mix well.

Tip: If you prefer, you can squeeze lime juice and top with cheese.

Serving suggestion: Serve it as a complete meal and immediately.

Mexican Buddha Bowl

Prep Time:	10 minutes	Calories:	311
Cook Time:	0 minutes	Fat (g):	12
Total Time:	10 minutes	Protein (g):	10
Servings:	4	Net carbs:	41

This buddha bowl can be an amazing and healthy bowl that contains quinoa, avocados, and many other superfoods.

Ingredients:

- Quinoa — 1 bag
- Black beans — 1 can
- Baby spinach — 1 bag
- Sliced avocados — Two
- Diced tomatoes — Two
- Corn — 1 cup
- Diced red onion — ¼
- Sliced jalapenos — 1
- Quartered lime — 1
- Cilantro, chopped — ½ cup
- Salt, pepper and Mexican spices — To taste

Instructions:

1. Equally, divide spinach among four bowls.
2. Add in quinoa, black beans, avocado, tomato, corn, red onion, and jalapeno in each bowl.
3. Sprinkle salt, pepper, and all Mexican spices to taste.
4. Garnish with cilantro and lime.

Tip: This bowl contains vegetables, but you can use grilled chicken or shrimp for a meat addition.

Serving suggestion: Serve it as the main meal with sour cream or Greek yogurt.

Mexican Meatloaf

Prep Time:	15 minutes	Calories:	149
Cook Time:	1 hour	Fat (g):	6
Total Time:	1 hour 15 minutes	Protein (g):	21
Servings:	6	Net carbs:	6

Mexican meatloaf is a classy dinner time meal with special Mexican taco seasoning.

Ingredients:

- Ground beef — 1 pound
- Breadcrumbs — ¼ cup
- Egg — 1
- Taco seasoning — 1 packet
- Tomatoes with chilies — 1 can
- Mexican cheese — ½ cup

Instructions:

1. Mix meat with seasoning, egg, and breadcrumbs.
2. Shape meat in loaf and place on a baking sheet.
3. Preheat oven to 350 F.
4. Pour drained tomatoes over meat.
5. Bake the meatloaf for 1 hour and take out.
6. Serve as it is or with cheese.

Tip: You can sprinkle with cheese and bake for 4-5 minutes more or until cheese melts.

Serving suggestion: Serve it as a complete meal with grated cheese.

Mexican DIY Burrito Bowls

Prep Time:	10 minutes	Calories:	525
Cook Time:	1 hour 30 minutes	Fat (g):	13
Total Time:	1 hour 40 minutes	Protein (g):	37
Servings:	4	Net carbs:	71

Design your burrito bowl with your favorite items and enjoy the healthy lunch.

Ingredients:

<u>For chicken</u>

• Boneless chicken thighs	1 pound
• Chucky salsa	1 cup
• Chipotle chili powder	½ tsp

<u>For rice</u>

• Coconut oil	2 tsp
• Short grain brown rice	1 cup
• Water	2 cups
• Lime juice	1 lime

<u>For corn salsa</u>

• Sweet corn	1 cup
• Red onion, diced	One
• Chopped cilantro	¼ cup
• Lime, juiced	One
• Salt and pepper	To taste

<u>For beans</u>

• Black or green beans of your choice, cooked	15 ounces

<u>For garnish</u>

• Shredded cheddar cheese	½ cup
• Extra salsa, avocado slices, sliced tomatoes, purple cabbage, green onions, eggs, Greek yogurt, hot sauce, etc.	

Instructions:

1. Bake chicken with chili powder and salsa in a preheated oven at 400 F for 20-25 minutes. Take out and cut the chicken in cubes or shred it.
2. Cook rice in a pot with oil for 5 mins. After 5 mins, add water and let simmer on low heat for 45 mins. Remove from heat and season with lime juice, salt, and pepper.
3. In a bowl, combine all salsa ingredients and set aside.
4. Make the bowls by distributing rice, beans, corn salsa, and chicken and garnish with desired items.

Tip: You can add more vegetables to it if you want to. Shrimp can be a good substitute for chicken.

Serving suggestion: Serve it as the main meal for dinner.

Mexican Flatbread

Prep Time:	5 minutes	Calories:	390
Cook Time:	10 minutes	Fat (g):	26
Total Time:	15 minutes	Protein (g):	16
Servings:	4	Net carbs:	26

Bringing salsa to a recipe is the Mexican style, and it is perfect for bringing on a flatbread with mayonnaise.

Ingredients:

• Flatbread or naan	1
• Chicken breast, sliced	One
• Corn or pepper mix	½ cup
• Black beans	½ cup
• Avocados	Half
• Tomato	Half
• Mayonnaise	½ cup
• Olive oil	3 tbsp
• Salt	½ tsp
• Chili lime hot sauce	3 tbsp

Instructions:

1. Sprinkle salt and pepper on chicken and cook it in a pan with oil.
2. Remove and dice it.
3. Place chicken, corn, beans, avocado, and tomatoes over the flatbread.
4. Heat in oven for 5-10 minutes at 350 F.
5. Make the sauce by mixing mayo with olive oil, salt, and hot sauce.
6. Pour over flatbread and enjoy.

Tip: Top it with rose petals for beauty. You can use cheese if you want.

Serving suggestion: Serve it as the main meal with your favorite soda drink.

Mexican Shrimp Tacos

Prep Time:	15 minutes	Calories:	453
Cook Time:	5 minutes	Fat (g):	21
Total Time:	20 minutes	Protein (g):	31
Servings:	4	Net carbs:	48

Enjoy amazing shrimp tacos with some corn tortillas and have the best lunchtime.

Ingredients:

- Corn tortillas — 12
- Avocados — Two
- Lime — 1, quartered
- Diced tomatoes — Two
- Salt — ½ tsp
- Onion — One
- Green leaf lettuce — 1 head
- Corn oil — ½ tbsp
- Shrimp, peeled and halved lengthwise — 1 pound
- Chili powder — 1 tsp
- Cumin — ½ tsp

Instructions:

1. Preheat oven to 325 F. Wrap tortillas in foil and place in oven.
2. Pit avocados and dice in small pieces. Squeeze lime juice over them and add in tomatoes and salt and mix to combine.
3. Chop onions and place in a small bowl. Slice lettuce into small strips and place in another bowl.
4. Heat oil in a skillet and cook shrimp with chili powder and cumin. Transfer to a bowl when done. Take out tortillas from the oven.
5. Serve with shrimp, lettuce, avocado and tomato mixture, and onions.

Tip: If you prefer, you can use sour cream or yogurt.

Serving suggestion: Serve it as a complete meal and immediately.

Corn and Chorizo Chowder

Prep Time:	10 minutes	Calories:	390
Cook Time:	40 minutes	Fat (g):	16
Total Time:	50 minutes	Protein (g):	18
Servings:	6	Net carbs:	44

Enjoy corn and chorizo chowder with some tasty flavors and spices.

Ingredients:

- Leeks	Two
- Yellow onion, chopped	1 cup
- Minced garlic clove	One
- Chorizo, sliced	6 ounces
- All-purpose flour	2 tbsp
- Russet potatoes, cubes	two
- Chicken stock	2 cups
- Water	2 cups
- Thyme	1 tsp
- Parsley	3 tbsp
- Salt and pepper	To taste
- Milk	1 ½ cups
- Corn	2 cups

Instructions:

1. Add leeks, garlic, onion, and chorizo in the pot and cook for 5 minutes. Sprinkle flour and stir for 1-2 minutes.
2. Add in potatoes and stock with water and cook on low heat for 10 minutes.
3. Add in thyme and parsley and season with salt and pepper and cook for 10 minutes on low until potatoes are tender.
4. Add milk and corn and cook uncovered for 5-10 minutes.

Tip: You can use more ingredients like onion, beans, or tomatoes if you want.

Serving suggestion: Serve it as a complete meal.

Mexican Frittata

Prep Time:	20 minutes	Calories:	310
Cook Time:	15 minutes	Fat (g):	20
Total Time:	35 minutes	Protein (g):	23
Servings:	4	Net carbs:	12

This is an easy and versatile recipe for making Mexican frittata, which is full of amazing ingredients.

Ingredients:

- Eggs — Ten
- Potato — One
- Chorizo sausage link — One
- Onion — Half
- Jalapenos — Two
- Chopped cilantro — ½ cup
- Jack cheese, cubes — ½ cup
- Shredded cotija cheese — ¼ cup
- Chipotle powder — ½ tsp
- Salt — ½ tsp
- Black pepper — To taste
- Olive oil — 1 tbsp

Instructions:

1. Crumble the chorizo with onion and jalapeno.
2. Cube the potatoes and add to salted boiling water and boil for 4-5 minutes. Drain and set aside.
3. Chop half an onion and 2 jalapenos and sauté in a dollop of oil for 6-8 minutes.
4. Add the chopped chorizo link and cook. Add in potatoes and season with salt and pepper and add cotija cheese. Combine well and add in the egg mixture.

5. Settle the eggs in a pan and add in cubed cheese and a layer of shredded cheese. Once cooked, slice up and serve.

Tip: Store the leftover in an airtight jar and keep in the refrigerator.

Serving suggestion: Serve it as a main meal in bowls along with the hot sauce.

Mexican Chicken and Rice

Prep Time:	15 minutes	Calories:	434
Cook Time:	35 minutes	Fat (g):	13
Total Time:	50 minutes	Protein (g):	29
Servings:	5	Net carbs:	50

Make with chicken and season this Mexican rice and enjoy the best.

Ingredients:

- Chicken thighs and legs — Five
- Diced yellow onion — One
- Garlic powder — 1 tsp
- Chili powder — 1 tbsp
- Ground cumin — 1 tsp
- Dried oregano — 1 tsp
- Paprika — ¼ tsp
- Salt — 1 tsp
- Cayenne — ¼ tsp
- Minced garlic — 1 tbsp
- Olive oil — 2 tbsp
- Uncooked white rice — 1 cup
- Chicken stock — 2 cups
- Salsa — 1 cup
- Red bell pepper, minced — ½ cup
- Parsley for garnish

Instructions:

1. Preheat oven to 350 F.
2. Season chicken with salt, garlic powder, chili powder, cumin, paprika, oregano, and cayenne. Add chicken in an iron skillet and cook until brown.
3. Flip and cook for 3-4 minutes more.

4. Place chicken on a plate. Add olive oil in a skillet and add in onions and cook for 3-4 mins. Add in garlic, rice, bell pepper, and salsa and cook until boil.
5. Add in chicken stock and place chicken back. Bake for 35-40 minutes.

Tip: Make this recipe with boneless chicken if you prefer.

Serving suggestion: Serve it as a complete meal with a crispy green salad.

Mexican Hotdogs

Prep Time:	10 minutes	Calories:	375
Cook Time:	10 minutes	Fat (g):	25
Total Time:	20 minutes	Protein (g):	13
Servings:	8	Net carbs:	27

These hot dogs are grilled topped with jalapenos, cheese, salsa, and sour cream. It is a crowd-pleaser.

Ingredients:

- Hot dogs	2 packages
- Taco seasoning	1 package
- Olive oil	½ cup
- Jalapeno pepper, sliced	Four
- Salsa	½ cup
- Mexican cheese	1 cup
- Sour cream	½ cup
- Avocados	Two

Instructions:

1. Preheat grill at medium heat.
2. In a bowl, mix taco seasoning and olive oil. Brush on hot dogs and coat well. Place them in the bottom rack of grill and cook for about 10 minutes.
3. Once cooked, take out and place on a plate.
4. Brush the buns and place on grill for a minute. Once done, place hot dogs in buns. Top each bun with peppers, salsa, avocados, cream, cheese, and cilantro.

Tip: Adjust salt as per your desire. You can use serrano peppers for a spicy flavor.

Serving suggestion: Serve it as the main meal for dinner.

Mexican Summer Couscous

Prep Time:	10 minutes	Calories:	346
Cook Time:	10 minutes	Fat (g):	2
Total Time:	20 minutes	Protein (g):	9
Servings:	4	Net carbs:	53

This is fresh, light, and healthiest couscous you will ever eat.

Ingredients:

- Red bell pepper, diced — One
- Orange or yellow bell pepper — Two
- Cranberries — ½ cup
- Strawberries, cut in segments — 1 cup
- Chopped cilantro — ¼ cup
- Three limes — Three
- Gluten-free couscous — 1 1/3 cup
- Salt — ½ tsp
- Oil of choice — 1 tbsp

Instructions:

1. Place 2 cups of water in a pan and add salt and oil. Boil it then add in couscous, cover and remove from heat.
2. In a bowl, mix peppers, cranberries, strawberries, and cilantro. Juice the limes over the mixture.

Tip: Top with tomatoes and green onions.

Serving suggestion: Serve it as a complete meal and squeeze extra lime juice, if needed.

Mexican Pozole

Prep Time:	40 minutes	Calories:	426
Cook Time:	10 hours	Fat (g):	25
Total Time:	10 hours 4 minutes	Protein (g):	28
Servings:	8	Net carbs:	22

This slow cooker Mexican pozole is one of the most delicious dishes from the region. You can make it at home with some simple steps to follow.

Ingredients:

- Hominy — 50 ounces
- Garlic cloves — Eight
- Fresh pork belly — 3 ½ pounds
- Chicken broth — 8 cups
- Diced onions — Two
- Guajillo peppers — 6
- Ancho peppers — 6
- Cumin — 1 tbsp
- Chili powder — 1 tbsp
- Mexican oregano — 2 tsp
- Salt, to taste

Instructions:

1. Toast the dried peppers in a skillet for a few minutes. Add in chilies and cover with 4 cups of water. Now let it simmer for 30 minutes and then turn off the heat to let cool.
2. In a blender, add 1 cup chili water, peppers, cumin, and garlic puree and make a smooth paste.
3. Strain out the seeds using a mesh strainer. The sauce is ready.
4. In the slow cooker, add onions, red sauce, chili powder, oregano, and pork belly. Cook on low heat for 8-10 hours. Once it is done, remove the pork and shred it. Now turn the slow cooker to high and add the hominy in it with the shredded pork.

5. Let it sit for a half-hour, and once it is warm, add salt to serve.

Tip: If you prefer, you can use avocado along with lime and radishes for topping.

Serving suggestion: Serve it as a complete meal and immediately with tortilla chips.

Mexican Chili-Lime Beef

Prep Time:	5 minutes	Calories:	650
Cook Time:	8 hours	Fat (g):	39
Total Time:	8 hours 5 minutes	Protein (g):	65
Servings:	4	Net carbs:	19

Make this Mexican style beef in your slow cooker and enjoy the amazing taste.

Ingredients:

- Beef chuck roast   2 pounds
- Lemon-lime soda   4 cups
- Chili powder   1 tsp
- Salt   1 tsp
- Crushed garlic cloves   Three
- Limes juiced   two

Instructions:

1. In a slow cooker, add beef and pour soda over the beef.
2. Season with chili powder, garlic, and salt.
3. Cover the pot and cook on low for 8 hours.
4. Take out and pour lime juice.

Tip: You can shred the beef if you want.

Serving suggestion: Serve it as a complete meal with avocados or sour cream.

Mexican Rotisserie Pizza

Prep Time:	10 minutes	Calories:	200
Cook Time:	5 minutes	Fat (g):	4
Total Time:	15 minutes	Protein (g):	6
Servings:	4	Net carbs:	36

Use the rotisserie chicken and refried beans and make the best Mexican pizza.

Ingredients:

- Low fat refried beans — 16 ounces
- Shredded rotisserie chicken — 2 cups
- Salsa — ½ cup
- Cooking spray
- Flour tortillas — Eight
- Red enchilada sauce — 5 ounces
- Shredded Mexican blend cheese — 8 ounces
- Green onions — 2
- Roma tomatoes — 2

Instructions:

1. Preheat oven to 350 F.
2. Warm beans and salsa/chicken mixture separately in the microwave.
3. Heat oil in a pan and fry tortilla from both sides.
4. Place four of the tortillas on a baking sheet and spread 2 tbsp refried beans on each. Top with salsa/chicken mixture and then other tortillas.
5. Spread over the layer of enchilada sauce and sprinkle cheese and tomatoes. Bake for 5-8 minutes and serve.

Tip: If you prefer, you can sprinkle the chopped cilantro and green onions.

Serving suggestion: Serve it as the main meal for dinner and immediately.

Mexican Corn Bread

Prep Time:	10 minutes	Calories:	180
Cook Time:	45 minutes	Fat (g):	9
Total Time:	55 minutes	Protein (g):	4
Servings:	4	Net carbs:	19

With some simple ingredients make this cornbread in a bread loaf pan or a bowl.

Ingredients:

- Self-rising cornmeal	2 cups
- Cream style corn	1 can
- Grated cheddar cheese	1 cup
- Jalapeno, chopped	Three
- Cooking oil	½ cup
- Salt	1 dash
- Buttermilk	½ cup

Instructions:

1. Preheat oven to 425 F.
2. In a bowl, mix all ingredients.
3. Pour the mixture in an iron skillet and bake for 30-45 minutes.

Tip: You can use a bread loaf pan for baking.

Mexican Cheese Vegetable Chowder

Prep Time:	10 minutes	Calories:	162
Cook Time:	10 minutes	Fat (g):	11
Total Time:	20 minutes	Protein (g):	8
Servings:	4	Net carbs:	8

This is fresh, light, and the healthiest cheese chowder made with vegetables and spices.

Ingredients:

- Butter — 3 tbsp
- Chopped carrots — 1 cup
- Sliced celery — 1 cup
- Diced onion — One
- Diced bell pepper — 1 cup
- Frozen corn — 1 cup
- Cumin — ½ tsp
- Chili powder — ½ tsp
- Chicken broth — 3 cups
- Milk — 2 cups
- Flour — 1/3 cup
- Mexican shredded cheese — 3 cups
- Chopped cilantro — 2 tbsp
- Salt and pepper — To taste

Instructions:

1. In a pan, melt butter and add in carrots, onion, celery, and bell pepper. Sauté for 5 mins and add in corn, cumin, chili powder, salt, and pepper.
2. Sauté for 2-3 mins. Pour in chicken broth and simmer over medium heat for 20 minutes.
3. Mix milk and flour and add in soup. Then add in cheese and cilantro.
4. Cook until cheese is melted and remove for serving.

Tip: Top with cilantro and green onions. You can sprinkle some cheese.

Hello,

This is Michael Walson. I would like to thank you for your interest in purchasing my book.

I hope that you are completely satisfied with the book you have purchased.

So what do you think about it? Is it awesome or lack somewhere?

For me, every customer is valuable, and your customer experience could really help me. I always go through great lengths to create my books of the best quality and meet your expectations. You can help me exceed your expectations by sharing your valuable opinions on my book. Your thoughts will provide me an opportunity to improve my book and make it looks better. Also, your words will help our potential buyers to make their minds for the purchase of this book.

I would really appreciate it if you could spare two minutes to rate this purchase.

Here's a little token of appreciation for you – you can join our social groups, where we always try to post the most yummies recipes:

Facebook group

Instagram group

Along with this, if you find anything wrong with the book, please get in touch with me directly at **headway.company3@gmail.com**, so that I have an opportunity to fix your issues.

Thank you in advance for your valuable feedback.

I hope you will enjoy it!

Kind regards,

Michael Walson

Made in the USA
Middletown, DE
11 May 2020

93954001R00071